VISION PLANNING – The Key to the Future

A Manual

Clifford Holliday

VISION PLANNING – The Key to the Future
A Manual

Written August, 2018

Copyright © 2018

Cover Design by Alice Holliday
Edited by Alice Holliday

All rights reserved. This includes, but is not limited to, the right to reproduce or extract any portion of this book in any form with out the author's permission.

First Edition: August, 2018-08-17

ISBN-10: 1725595478
ISBN-13: 978-1725595477

This book is dedicated to my lovely wife, Alice Holliday, who has not only provided her artistic ability to design my cover and help edit the text, but has also been very gracious regarding my long absences while preparing the book.

Clifford Holliday

Table of Contents

Table of Contents .... - 4 -
Table of Figures .... - 6 -
INTRODUCTION .... - 7 -
    Using This Manual .... - 10 -
Lesson 1 – ESTABLISHING THE PLANNING FRAMEWORK ...... - 13 -
    Lesson Outline .... - 13 -
    Prerequisites for this lesson. .... - 13 -
    Lesson Introduction .... - 14 -
    The Planning Model .... - 15 -
        Vision Planning Direction – Example I .... - 17 -
        Vision Planning Direction – Example II .... - 18 -
        Strategic Planning – Example Statement .... - 19 -
        Implementation – Example Statement .... - 20 -
        Things to do in this Lesson. .... - 22 -
        Assignments for the next lesson. .... - 22 -
Lesson 2 – UNDERSTANDING VISION PLANNING .... - 23 -
    Lesson Outline .... - 23 -
    Prerequisites for this lesson. .... - 23 -
    Lesson Introduction .... - 23 -
        Learning from the Example .... - 26 -
    Development of a Vision .... - 26 -
        Example of Vision Statement -- IBM's New Vision and Associated Goals .... - 27 -
        Learning from the Example .... - 28 -
    The Vision Planning Pyramid .... - 29 -
    The Vision Planning Process .... - 31 -
        Assignments for the next lesson. .... - 34 -
Lesson 3 – HOW TO DO VISION PLANNING .... - 35 -
    Lesson Outline .... - 35 -
    Prerequisites for this lesson. .... - 35 -
    Lesson Introduction .... - 35 -
    Step 1. Vision statement .... - 36 -
    Step 2. Developing a view of the future and testing the vision ... - 39 -
        Learning from the Example .... - 46 -
        Things to do in this lesson. .... - 46 -
        Assignments for the next lesson. .... - 47 -
4.   Lesson 4 – INTEGRATING VISION PLANNING .... - 49 -
    Lesson Outline .... - 49 -
    Prerequisites for this lesson. .... - 49 -

Vision Planning – A Key to the Future

Lesson introduction ....- 50 -
How Is Vision Planning Different from Strategic Planning? ....- 50 -
    Lincoln Vision Example – Continued ....- 50 -
    Revised Planning Model ....- 53 -
    Revised Model ....- 55 -
Integration Example – School District ....- 57 -
    Learning from the Example ....- 58 -
Summary ....- 59 -
    Things to do in this lesson. ....- 60 -
Endnotes ....- 61 -

Table of Figures

FIGURE 1. THE PLANNING MODEL ....- 16 -
FIGURE 2. THE VISION PLANNING PYRAMID ....- 31 -
FIGURE 3. THE VISION PLANNING APPROACH ....- 31 -
FIGURE 4. THE TRADITIONAL PLANNING APPROACH................- 32 -
FIGURE 5. VISIONING PROCESS ....- 37 -
FIGURE 6, ORIGINAL PLANNING MODEL......................................- 54 -
FIGURE 7. PLANNING MODEL WITH VISION PLANNING
  EXPANDED ....- 56 -

Vision Planning – A Key to the Future

INTRODUCTION

This manual deals primarily with Vision Planning, what it is; how to organize for it; and how to do it. This process is much more than what is commonly thought of as strategic planning. It is, rather, a recurring and defining planning thread that runs through the entire corporate entity. This process (rather than the actual plans) allows an organization to cope with rapid changes in its environment. The process produces strategic plans; provides for the orderly implementation of these plans to meet organizational objectives; and institutionalizes an ongoing feedback process to allow continual measurement of results. **This process allows organizations to become 'designers of the future', rather than passive victims.**

The focus is on how to develop an organizational 'Vision', and the elements necessary to achieve integration of that vision as a driving force with the other essential elements of planning. The 'lessons' take an almost cookbook approach to the important sub-elements in Vision Planning and each of their relationships to the overall planning effort.

This manual is designed so that it may be used in multiple ways:

- As a learning tool to simple explore the concept and application of Vision planning.
- As a guide for a teacher introducing implementing Vision Planning.
- As a student workbook for use in a Vision Planning course.

This manual provides a detailed outline to assist an organization in understanding the concepts of Vision Planning, why they are important, and how that set of concepts can be used in the organization's own planning model. (While it is directed towards a business environment and terms like 'company' or 'enterprise' may often be used, it is intended for any kind of an organization.) This manual will present a series of 'lessons' that can be used either as a stand-alone resource guide, or in conjunction with a consultant/facilitator/guide.[i]

It should be noted that the subject of Vision Planning is treated in a generic sense. While much of the example and case material is taken from a background in the telecommunications industry, it is intended that the material can be generalized to many industries and many different types of organizations. As the information is developed, generalization examples are included so that this information can be applied to a broad range of environments. Given the importance of processing and communications in today's world of re-engineering (and the cross - industry prevalence of re-engineering) a 'bias' in the direction of computing and communications technology is unavoidable.

The concepts included herein were developed through the use of material developed by the leading researchers and writers in business and organizational behavior; through observing the lessons of history; and through the application, modification and extension of these works and observations based on the author's extensive planning experience. This manual enhances the previously published material by providing a logically consistent integration of the ideas of Vision Planning and by establishing a specific framework that can be used as a direct pattern for implementing these concepts in any organization.

Vision Planning – A Key to the Future

The primary researchers (although by no means the only ones) influencing this approach are Tom Peters and Thomas Davenport. The sources from history are many and varied, but many military writers tend to offer the greatest insights. The background of the author that is applicable to this work includes: (1) the author's 30+ years in the technical, operations and business planning organizations of a major telecommunications carrier; (2) his time spent as a planning consultant to the electrical power (alternative fuels) industry; and (3) most recently, through his decades as a planning consultant and analyst to the telecommunications industry and its customers.

The approaches described in this Manual are not a simple re-count of any single company's practices, or of any particular writer. Rather, they are an amalgamation of practices used by various companies and other organizations as well as practices described in the literature and which the author has used or seen used as a consultant to the energy, education and telecommunications sectors. This mix has been developed in to a straight forward template for converting an organization's planning process to one based on the Vision concept of driving, rather than being driven by, future events.

The following lessons are included in this manual;

Lesson 1 – Establishing the Planning Framework – This lesson will start by trying to help the organization evaluate the existing planning process. This is meant to be a 'scene-setting' exercise for the following lessons on Vision Planning.

Lesson 2 – Understanding Vision Planning - This lesson addresses formalizing the definition of, and developing an understanding of, Vision Planning and vision development. It is intended that this understanding will allow application to generalized business situations as well as to problems of everyday life.

Lesson 3 – How to Do Vision Planning – This lesson initiates the concept of Vision Planning as a process. It provides an in-depth review of each of the four steps of the Vision Planning process.

Lesson 4 – Integrating Vision Planning - This lesson will focus on how to integrate the Vision Planning concepts in to the organization's planning structure. This work will be organization specific, and will focus on implementing the vision planning process in the user's organization.

In addition to the text, each Lesson includes 'sidebars' ('Lesson Outline', 'Prerequisites for this Lesson' and 'Things to Do in this Lesson') to aid the team leader. Each of the first three lessons also includes specific 'Assignments for the Next Lessons', which provides preparatory activities for each participant before the next meeting.

Using This Manual

It is intended that these lessons be conducted over a period of time. However, it is recognized that the urgencies of organizational needs may not always offer that luxury. This material has thus been arranged so that it has a flexibility of application. Some of the ways it can be used are:
- One per week (about 3-4 hours each) for four weeks – probably the optimal arrangement
- One per day for most of a week
- As a two day retreat (a very busy one)

The set of lessons (see above for a description of each) consists of the first planning overview session plus three sessions on Vision Planning. Lesson 3 has a great deal of material in it and may be split in to two parts (recommend it be split after the part on Vision statements.)

A team should be carefully selected for these lessons. It is important that the results of the overall exercise are taken as

Vision Planning – A Key to the Future

an important change in the way the organization is to be run. For this reason, the composition of the team is critical. This composition should be such that its determinations will be widely accepted throughout the organization. The team must be broad enough to represent, at a high level, all-important segments of the organization, and it also must be perceived as powerful enough in the organization to implement the results. Examples of composition would include an organization's president (CEO) and his direct reports, or the president, his top planners, and selected leaders of operational parts of the organization. It is, of course, essential that the individual, who is to have the responsibility for implementing the results (and the individual to have ongoing ownership of the process) be a member of the team.

In setting the team size the normal constraints of team size should be considered. The team should be big enough to include all of the important 'constituencies' of the organization, but small enough to function in a team interactive mode. A target size of around 6 to 8 is likely optimal, with a top limit of around 15. The team will need the normal, minimal support resources of a task force of this size.

The head of the organization should, at least, start the proceedings. It would be ideal if he/she personally led each session. In cases where this is not possible, a leader should be appointed who is directly responsible to the organization head for this effort.

The leader should use a facilitator (either consultant or in-house, if a properly qualified person is available) to help keep the meetings on target and moving.
A 'Lesson Outline' is provided for each lesson. The leader can use this to review at the end of the meeting to assure that all topics have been covered.

A list of 'Prerequisites' for the lessons is provided. This list is to help in assuring that all of the preliminary activities have been considered.

A 'Things to Do in This Lesson' box is provided in each Lesson as a guide to the leader in the activities that will help lead to the needed discussions, learning and the resultant actions for each lesson.

While this manual is set up primarily to use as an agent of change in an organization's planning process, it may also be used as an indoctrination tool. Thus for example, if new members are added to the board, or if the understanding of the process needs to be extended, it can be used in those contexts.

Vision Planning – A Key to the Future

Lesson 1 – ESTABLISHING THE PLANNING FRAMEWORK

Lesson Outline

Why is planning important?

What does a 'Planning Model' look like?

What is the planning model of our organization?

How does this generalized model fit to our organization?

How can the model be modified to make it better fit our company?

Should we change our model?

Prerequisites for this lesson.

(_Planning must be perceived as important to the health and wealth of the organization. Every communication about a review of planning approaches and techniques must convey this message of importance. If this perception is not conveyed and believed, the effort is not worth the time._)

An announcement of the intention to seriously review the organization's planning approach.

An appointment of members (and a public announcement) of the planning study by the head (CEO, chairman, president, or appropriate personage) of the organization.

A call by the organization's head to the first meeting, with a clear message of the importance of attendance and participation.

All attendees should review the first lesson material, prior to the meeting.

Lesson Introduction

There have been many books and articles written about the exercise of planning in the corporate environment. Even books written about other aspects of the firm often include extensive material about planning. While this proliferation provides many sources, it also provides for a source of confusion. Ideas such as vision, quality, strategy, values, etc. are introduced in these sources. There is a tendency for each of these authors to develop some of these concepts to illustrate the aspect of planning that is of interest to his thesis. Unfortunately, this leaves the impression that he has represented the totality of planning, while that is often not the case. Planning is seldom treated as a process and it is unusual for it to be presented in a 'how-to' format.

This manual deals primarily with Vision Planning, what it is; how to organize for it; and how to do it. However, in order to avoid the trap alluded to above, the first lesson will deal with an overview of the planning process. This process is much more than what is commonly thought of as strategic planning. It is, rather, the recurring and defining thread that runs through the entire corporate entity. This process (rather than the actual plans) allows an organization to cope with rapid changes in the environment. The process produces strategic plans and provides for the orderly implementation of these plans to meet organizational objectives.

General Eisenhower appreciated and identified the importance of the process. He expressed it most eloquently, "In preparing for battle I have always found that plans are useless, but planning is indispensable." (Dwight D. Eisenhower (1890-1969). This was one of Eisenhower's favorite maxims.)

Vision Planning – A Key to the Future

The Planning Model

A model will be developed in this chapter that will be used in later lessons. This model will consist of three significant parts: vision, strategy and implementation. It will not however be a linear model, but rather it will turn back upon itself to form a circle by connecting to a fourth activity that we call 'direction'.

This model looks like Figure 1 in its simplest form. A planning model for a specific organization should contain more detail (ultimately – but start with a simple representation). The added detail should include such items as:

- Internal organization identification names
- Major inputs and outputs (documents)
- Time frames

Clifford Holliday

THE PLANNING MODEL

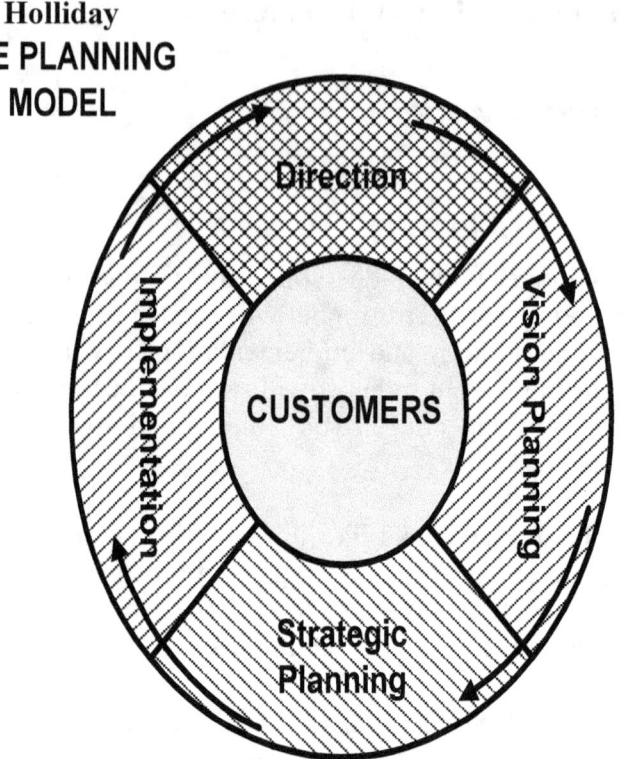

(C) 1998 B & C Consulting Services

Figure 1. The Planning Model

  The Planning Model is a circular chain that runs through the entire corporate entity. It starts with overall direction, develops a vision and then develops strategies intended to cause the realization of the desired future. It is the integrating element

in the tactical plans and in the implementation of the tactics. It is the basis and the benchmark for the oversight and direction of the entire process. This brings the process back to the beginning

Vision Planning – A Key to the Future

of the chain and includes a constant updating of the vision, the strategies, the tactical plans and finally the implementation approaches. This process provides the basis for making consistent decisions, even in the face of a rapidly changing environment. It should be noted that the entire process circulates around the customer. In developing these processes, the focus must be kept on the customer (sometimes in the context of 'future customer') at all times.

Vision Planning Direction – Example I

"This company will become a CLEC (Competitive Local Exchange Carrier)."

This is the starting point of the planning continuum. It comes from many places, not necessarily just the top of the organization. In order to be useful 'Direction' must present a clear and non-contradictory set of objectives or goals for the organization. The danger in many organizations is that direction is coming from many different locations within and with out the organization. These different entities will likely have different internal perspectives and different agendas. Such a 'multi-direction' environment will result in a contradictory set of goals and will pre-doom any planning effort – no matter how good the planning technique.

An example of this multi-direction confusion can be seen in many large companies. Typically, the staff and major line subdivisions will have enough resources to establish 'directions' that are based on their particular view of the world rather than the overall needs of the organization. One can easily imagine how Marketing, Engineering and Operating Departments would see the world differently, and how different their individual perceptions may be as to appropriate directions.

An early necessity in establishing a workable planning process is to define an appropriate source of direction – usually this needs to be the main job of the head of the organization.

Vision Planning Direction – Example II

"We will be a facilities based CLEC (Competitive Local Exchange Company) in Texas using a new wireless local loop technology."

This revised direction statement is much more specific in that it provides the desired location and the general methodology envisioned. This allows the planners to start with a much more specific set of parameters, and allows them to focus on the actual desired outcome (the future.) In a working Vision Planning organization, such a specific vision would not preclude a variance of either the location (e.g., including part of Oklahoma in the implementation) nor a different methodology, either in part or whole (e.g., using fiber in metro areas and wireless everywhere else.)

The concept of a driving vision for a corporation is becoming one of the fundamental precepts for the successful operation of a business in the world of today and tomorrow. A 'vision' is the company's view of a desired future at a very high level (i.e., at a very generalized level). It is not something that you get right the first time, nor is it something that requires perfect knowledge of the future, nor is it counter to flexibility. On a positive note, vision is a circular chain that runs through the entire organizational entity. In companies that properly use vision planning, it is the heart of the planning process. Vision provides the basis for making decisions based on a planning framework rather than in a reactive mode.

Intel is an example of a company with an obvious vision. If there were ever a clearer example of a company with a strong view of their desired future and with a clear corporate process to achieve that future, it is Intel. They have gone so far as to have shown us that process and to educate us as to its

Vision Planning – A Key to the Future

details in their (somewhat misnamed) advertisement – 'Intel Technology Briefings'.

The importance of understanding vision and its impact goes beyond the organization planning process. It truly is almost all pervasive in an organization's life. As an example, the selection of a vendor is often thought of as a somewhat mundane organizational function. However, in selecting a vendor one needs to select based on the vendor's vision as much as his current product. In this day of ever increasing competition, technology change, and rules (legal and otherwise) changes, one must have a firm basis on which to make vendor selections. The current state of product development is a very transitory criterion, and if followed blindly, can lead to chaos (of which there are many examples). A sound basis for such selections (often made under time constraints and in the face of a bewildering array of options) is a solid, consistent and well communicated corporate vision of the future.

Strategic Planning – Example Statement

"We will install five class 5G mobile service in the DFW Metroplex by 2020 in the following locations."

Strategic planning is the more traditional planning approach that defines (still at a high level, but with more detail than in a Vision Statement) actions for the next planning period – 5 years in some industries – and attaches the associated high-level financials to these plans. Too often, this process takes on a life of its own, without any real consideration of how the organization wants to change with the future or wants to change the future, i.e., it is not driven by Vision Planning. The trap with Strategic planning is to merely project the past to obtain future results. The surest result of such 'projection planning' is to be trapped in the past, and to become the victim of those more progressive organizations willing to take a part in establishing the future.

As will be seen in later lessons, an agreed on, understood and clear statement of the organization's vision must drive Strategic Planning. The function of Backward Deployment will be developed in that latter lesson, and the use of this concept to directly tie Vision to Strategic Planning and Implementation will become clear. Without this kind of direct tie, Strategic Planning is merely an accounting exercise of planning for the past.

Implementation – Example Statement

"We will cutover our first class 5G area in Plano on Dec 31, 2019, at 12:01 AM."

Implementation also involves planning. Anyone who has been responsible for implementation knows this involvement from first hand knowledge. This planning is often refereed to as Tactical Planning.

Tactical Planning

- In detail how will it be done?
- Who will do it?
- When will it be done (exactly)?
- What are the order, resource requirements and duration of individual events?

As with Strategic Planning, Implementation and Tactical Planning need to be clearly tied to the vision of the organization. Even an outsider should be able to clearly understand how the implementation activities are in direct support of the organization's Direction, Vision and Strategic Plan. The comparison of results of the Implementation to the

Vision Planning – A Key to the Future

outputs of the Vision Planning Process (specifically, the Backwards Deployment steps) provide a method for direct measurement of results.

Things to do in this Lesson.

Define (draw) your organization's planning model. Put names, inputs, outputs, and organizations on it.

How does your organization compare to the model in this lesson?

Determine where Direction comes from in your organization. (Suggestion: Have each participant write down his answer and then compare those on a chart.) Where did Direction come from in developing the last Strategic Plan?

Is there confusion or a multitude of contradictory goals represented by the current sources of Direction?

What is your organization's Vision? Ask each participant.

Discuss:
Who should set Direction?
Where (organizationally) would a Vision be developed?
How closely tied are your Implementation activities to your planning activities?
How does your organization measure planning success?

Assignments for the next lesson.

1. Develop a method to assure that Direction is consistent.
2. Suggest how a Vision should be developed.
3. Read the material for the next lesson.
4. Obtain and read a management organization book (any author – only the chapters about planning.)

Lesson 2 – UNDERSTANDING VISION PLANNING

Lesson Outline

People of Vision – some good, some bad.

What is Vision Planning?

Examples of Vision.

The Vision Planning Pyramid.

The difference between Vision Planning and Traditional Planning.

Prerequisites for this lesson.

Completion of the first lesson.

Completion of the Assignments from the last lesson (Lesson 1).

Review of the material for this lesson.

Lesson Introduction

History is replete with examples of men with uncommon vision and with the successes that they have achieved in terms of their vision. Some of these men we now call heroes and some we call scoundrels, it depends largely on what their vision entailed. For example, Lincoln is considered by many now to be one of the greatest presidents, while Hitler is considered one of the most evil men of all history. However, it is clear that they both were visionaries regarding the future of their respective countries and they were exceptionally successful in achieving their visions. (Of course, it is understood that some would argue that Hitler was not a success, because he was ultimately defeated and cost his country great losses. So did Lincoln! Although Lincoln was ultimately victorious, he also cost his country great loss – more Americans were killed in the Civil War than in any other. However, the historical and philosophical arguments aside, they both achieved their view of their countries' future. Hitler's just didn't last very long. (Thanks to General Patton and the 'Greatest Generation.')

Did they achieve this success by being able to foresee the future? No - they were designers of the future. They were able to influence future events to make them support their vision. How were they able to convert their views of the future in to reality? They made the conversion by having a clear view of what that future should be (Direction); by planning based on that view of the future (Vision); by planning and then acting consistently based on the vision (Strategic Planning and Implementation); and by having a defined feedback to provide on-going internal checks and measurements (back to Direction).

This lesson addresses formalizing the definition of, and developing an understanding of, Vision Planning and vision development. It is intended that this understanding will allow application to generalized business situations as well as to problems of everyday life.

What Is Vision Planning?

Vision Planning is, in the simplest terms, a set of goal development activities. Vision Planning is however, in the context of the overall Planning Model, much more than just

Vision Planning – A Key to the Future

goal setting. Vision Planning is the cornerstone on which everything else in the planning cycle is based.

Lincoln Civil War Example of Vision

Lincoln had a very clear vision throughout the Civil War, and he always planned and acted on that vision, in spite of many setbacks. Lincoln's vision was nothing to do with an invasion of the South, nor with military victories, nor with destroying the Southern armies, nor even with the ending of slavery. **It was rather the preservation of the Union**. He stated this at the beginning of the war, and clearly acted on it throughout the War. These other thoughts were strategies that he planned and acted on only as they were appropriate to achieving his vision.

Lincoln said early in the war, "This is essentially a people's contest. On the side of the Union, it is a struggle for maintaining in the world that form and substance of government whose leading object is to elevate the condition of men -- to lift artificial weights from all shoulders -- to clear the paths for laudable pursuit for all -- to afford all an unfettered start, and a fair chance, in the race of life."ii It can be seen that Lincoln's well know beliefs about the equality of man are interwoven in this statement of his vision, but he is unmistakably clear about the goal of the War, "... it is a struggle for maintaining in the world that form and substance of government..."

In the middle of the war, after having to change generals many times and having to change even the basic character of the war, Lincoln is still carrying this same message as found in the close of his most famous address in dedication of the new cemetery at Gettysburg, "... and that government of the people, by the people, for the people shall not perish from the earth."iii

Toward the end of the war in the presidential election year of 1864 Lincoln told the troops of the 166th Ohio

Regiment on a visit to the battlefield, "...for all time to come that we should perpetuate this great and free government ... for this the struggle should be maintained ... The nation is worth fighting for ..." These last comments were made to a group of soldiers who were likely going to be asked to risk death for Lincoln's vision of the perpetuation of the Union. They were also being asked to vote for him in the very critical election of 1864 (and at the time of the remarks, it was very unsure as to whether Lincoln could prevail over the peace candidate - General McClellan).

Learning from the Example

♦ Lincoln's vision was always clear and clearly stated. However, his generals did not always hear him. A Vision must be effectively communicated to be implemented.

♦ Lincoln's vision endured, even in the face of military and political adversity and in spite of the need for multiple strategies, to achieve the desired goal.

Development of a Vision

The first step in Vision Planning is the development of a vision of the future. For the leader of a business, this vision specifies (in a form that is concise, clear and actionable) the future for his business. Good vision statements seem easy to recognize because of the clarity and preciseness embodied in them. For example, "Our software will be preeminent in its field by the year 2020 as demonstrated by its use by at least five of the ten largest companies in the industry." This is clear, concise and measurable. Whether it is really a good vision statement depends on the difficulty of the task laid out. If four of the five companies targeted are already using their software, then it is a

Vision Planning – A Key to the Future

very complacent statement of goals and not a good vision statement. If, at the other end of the spectrum, it is known that the software will not be ready until late 2021, and that competitors will have products in the field in 2019, then it is also not a good vision statement. It is not good because it is unattainable, and no amount of focus or leadership is going to make it happen.

Vision statements are then a balance between what can be done and what is very difficult. They are developed through an iterative process that measures proposed statements against what is projected for the future. The details of developing a vision statement will be outlined in the next lesson.

Example of Vision Statement -- IBM's New Vision and Associated Goals

Before beginning the more detailed discussion of Vision Planning as a process in the next section of this lesson, it will be instructive to visit another example of the application of vision to an organization. IBM, that once unchallengeable of fortresses, experienced serious and successful challenges in almost every line of its business in the late 1980's and early 90's. On April 1, 1993, IBM took an unprecedented step in bringing in an outsider as the Chairman, when Louis V. Gerstner from RJR Nabisco was appointed to that post. Mr. Gerstner was a seasoned executive when he took over the ailing giant, but an early statement of his shocked many IBM watchers, "...a vision is the last thing IBM needs."iv

A year later, with IBM in apparently no better shape, Mr. Gerstner was ready with his new vision for IBM, "... to be the world's most important and successful information technology company." While this may not be the model of vision statements, it certainly does carry a message of the pursuit of excellence in the information industry.v The corollaries that Mr. Gerstner added to his vision statement facilitated a very important aspect to that statement -- the aspect of being actionable. Those corollaries were;

- Improve technology transfer from IBM's laboratories.
- Improve IBM's position in the technology of client – server.
- Participate in the building of the information superhighway.
- -Expanding IBM's stake in emerging markets.

This apparent change in heart by Mr. Gerstner seems to embody the beginning of a realization of the importance of vision planning in his strategic operations. It was also the beginning of IBM's return to being one of the world's most successful companies, which it has continued to be by being able to rapidly remake itself as its market and technology changed.

Learning from the Example
- Even when problems may seem related to short term problems such as adverse market conditions, competition, poor productivity, etc., the real culprit may well be a lack of vision.
- Vision statements may need expansion in order to allow implementation (in most cases).

The Vision Planning Pyramid

Vision Planning – A Key to the Future

This section will explore the Vision Planning process more closely to gain an in-depth understanding of the concept.

This work will prepare us to take the next step in the following lesson of applying these principles to Vision Planning in action.

The process of Vision Planning can easily be likened to a pyramid. It starts at the top of the organization with a very fine point (although the development of the information (direction) at the pyramid point may have involved more than the top of the organization), and it moves down the organization with an ever-widening base. The pyramid point is the draft vision statement itself. As one works down the pyramid, ever-increasing detail is developed as the vision is tested, restated, and moved toward realization.

The pyramid is represented in Figure 2. The top of the pyramid is the draft vision statement and the bottom is the high level planning for the programs and processes that will achieve the vision. The middle steps are the testing and revision stages designed to assure the feasibility of the vision. The next chapter will be devoted to the development of the details of each step of the Vision Planning process.

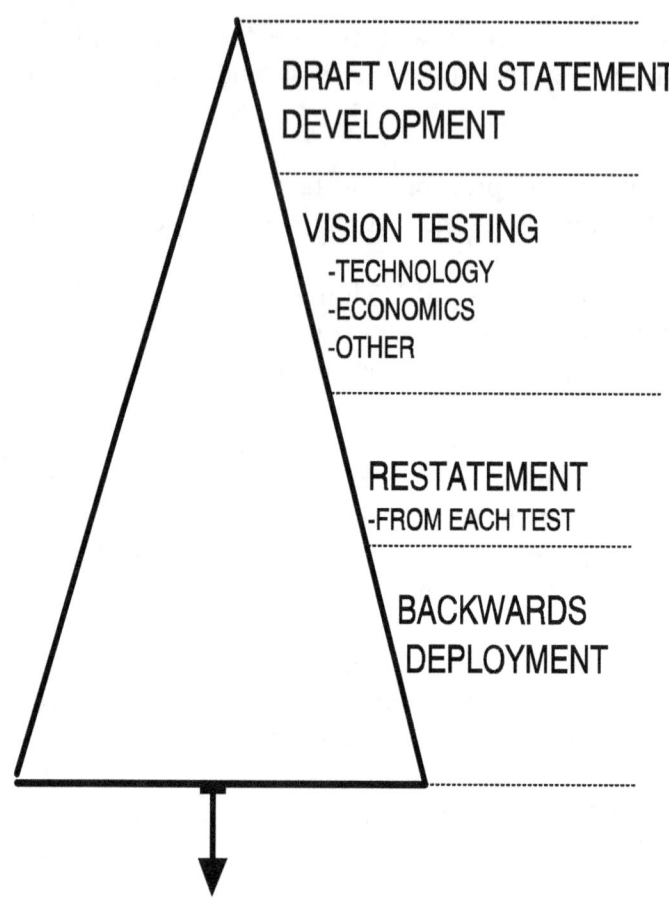

Figure 2. The Vision Planning Pyramid

The Vision Planning Process

This process begins with one's perception of a desired future based on personal experiences, training, temperament and all the other attributes that make up the whole person. The inputs of others are then added in a mix that has to be

Vision Planning – A Key to the Future

determined by the organization involved, by the nature of the vision, and ultimately by the individual developing the vision. This overall process can be described by Figure 3.

Vision Planning Approach

    I. Identify Overall Goal at Future Date
      (Draft Vision Statement)
    II Test Vision Statement
        - Against future market
        - Against future technology availability
        - Against present organization
    III Restate Vision Based on Tests
    IV Backwards Deployment

    Traditional Planning Stages

    V Develop Implementation Plans
    VI Implementation

Figure 3. The Vision Planning Approach

    The first four of these activities are the heart of Vision Planning. These four steps are directly from the pyramid in Figure 2. The remaining steps are from a traditional approach to planning.

    It is instructive to contrast this approach to the more traditional approach to planning that may follow an outline similar to the following Figure 4.

Traditional   Planning   Approach

    I. Identify Specific Situation
    II. Determine and Specify Problems in the Existing Situation
    III. Develop Alternatives to Correct One or More of the Problems
    IV. Utilize Appropriate Study Methods to Select Solution
    V. Develop Implementation Plans
    VI. Implement

Figure 4. The Traditional Planning Approach

The most striking difference is that **Vision Planning starts with the solution** (i.e., the Vision), while the **traditional approach starts with the problem**. Thus Vision Planning tends to start with a very high level view of the future, rather than risking becoming enamored with, and stuck in, today's problems. The Vision Planning approach encourages broad, imaginative thinking, and it discourages tunnel vision. On the other hand, the traditional approach often burdens the planner with so much detail about the current situation and problems, that he has a very difficult time focusing on the future.

The oft quoted story, "... it is difficult to concentrate on draining the swamp when the alligators are nipping at your heels..." is very appropriate in comparing Vision Planning to the more traditional approach. The traditional approach is perfectly geared to becoming expert at fighting the alligators, but if the company's goal is to farm the cleared and drained swamp, planning to kill the alligators looses focus on the real objective.

Vision Planning – A Key to the Future

Things to do in this Lesson.

Review Assignments from Lesson 1.

- What is the best way to assure consistency of Direction?
- Is this 'best' way doable in this organization? Why or Why Not?
- Review the answers to how a Vision should be developed.

Ask each participant to identify people of vision from their personal experience or from history.

Compare the steps of The Vision Planning Process to the process used in this organization (see Things To Do - Lesson 1).

Discuss:
- Where should an Organization's Vision come from?
- Where does it come from in this organization?
- What changes should be made in our approach?

Assignments for the next lesson.

1. Develop a method to fit the Vision Planning Pyramid in to this organization's Planning Process.
2. List three advantages of the Vision Planning Approach as opposed to the Traditional Planning Approach.
3. Is the concept of 'testing against the future' included in the current planning process? Should it be?
4. Develop a proposed Vision Statement for the organization.
5. Read the material for the next lesson.
6. Read the planning sections of another management organization book.

Lesson 3 – HOW TO DO VISION PLANNING

Lesson Outline

The steps of Vision Planning.

The Vision Statement.

What is a good vision statement?

Testing the Vision and Restatement.

Backwards Deployment.

Prerequisites for this lesson.

Completion of lessons 1 and 2.

Completion of assignments from Lesson 2.

Review of material for this lesson.

Lesson Introduction

Vision Planning – A Key to the Future

Let us begin this lesson with a look at each of the steps in developing the basis for a Vision Planning system:

- Vision Statement
- Testing
- Restatement
- Backwards Deployment

Step 1. Vision statement

Much has already been said about the development of the vision statement. It has been noted that it needs to be concise, clear, actionable, a 'stretch' but 'doable' and it needs to be the focus of the leader. Many authors have noted the attributes of a good vision statement. The following is a composite list:

1. Effective Visions are inspiring.

2. Effective visions are clear and challenging - and about excellence.

3. Effective visions make sense in the marketplace, and, by stressing flexibility and execution, stand the test of time in a turbulent world.

4. Effective visions must be stable but constantly challenged - and changed at the margin.

5. Effective visions are beacons and controls when all else is up for grabs.

6. Effective visions are aimed at empowering our own people first, customers second.

7. Effective visions prepare for the future, but honor the past.

8. Effective visions are lived in details, not in broad strokes.vi

Given these guidelines and the previous discussion the reader should have a comfortable feel of what makes a good vision, or at least how to recognize a good one when it is developed. But how does one go about actually developing a vision statement?

Again, various authors have provided us with a relatively structured approach to the development of a vision statement that may be more usable to the first time practitioner of the Vision Planning process. The composite is a procedure relatively heavy in terms of participation. This procedure recommends a series of workshops, the first being a brainstorming session in which a draft vision statement is developed. Each succeeding workshop is devoted to a refinement and restatement of the vision, while also adding detail (going down the pyramid). A series of questions (see Figure 5) can be used that would key each workshop after the first draft development session. As will be seen each of these is intended to provide the iterative approach to the vision development as well as bring more information in to the vision.

Figure 5. Visioning Process

Question	New Information
"How could we do things differently?"	Initial Vision Statement
"How will it work?"	Key Characteristics
"How well will it work?"	Measurements and Objectives
"What things have to go right?"	Critical Success Factors
"Why may those things not go right?"	Barriers to Success

Vision Planning – A Key to the Future

The establishment of an initial vision statement is clearly the most important part of the process. Exactly how it is done is not as important as doing it. The process is designed for rework
as each step unfolds, but there must be a starting point, and the preparation of a Vision Statement is that starting point.

Vision Statement Example – The 'Mascot Example'

Not all Visions are complex, or esoteric. One of the best Vision statements this author has ever heard was quite the opposite. It came out of a strategic planning meeting between a large communications carrier and a major, highly successful, entertainment company. The companies were interested in determining if there was common ground for some joint venture in bringing new entertainment to the home. To explore this possibility the meeting agenda included a review by each company of its strategies. The communications company went first and its strategic review consisted of many charts and graphs depicting projections, financial forecasts, and strategic initiatives. After the two hours or so of the communications company presentation, it was time for the entertainment company to make its presentation. One person came to the front of the room without slides or charts. He sat on the desk in the front and explained, "We really don't have material like that. Our vision is very simple. It is *'Keep the Mascot in Front of the People.'*"

A careful review of that entertainment company's practices shows that they do indeed "Keep the Mascot in Front of the People." He is in all their advertisements. He is etched on the sliding glass doors in your room if you stay in their hotels. He is on the bars of soap in their rest rooms. He is on the toilet paper. He is the most prominent of the 'characters' at any big event of theirs. If you talk to any one who works for them, he is uppermost in their mind. The mascot has been the symbol of their success for fifty years.

> **Learning from the Example**
>
> - Even in complex industries, Vision statements can be very simple, if they say enough.
> - The best Visions are extremely well communicated and understood.
> - Great Vision statements will stand the test of time. (That does not mean that review of subtending plans is unnecessary, but the Vision itself should be a long-term proposition.)

Step 2. Developing a view of the future and testing the vision

It is at this stage that the process begins to restrict the vision to what is feasible and realistic. This will be an activity of refining the vision and perhaps of taking some of the optimism out of the 'freethinking' that has gone into the vision development. While this and succeeding steps will be approaches to realism, it is paramount to remember that a vision must be challenging, and the leader must exercise that leadership by continually being the champion of the 'stretch'.

The draft vision has to be tested against many things -- market projections, anticipated customer needs, suspected competitor actions, and regulatory change. However, one of the most important, if not the most important at this early stage, is the test against technology projections. Citing this as the first test may be surprising to some, but if a vision is technologically infeasible then all else is secondary. If the technology required is not evaluated, there is no way to judge the other important yardsticks (cost, market, competitors, etc.).

Vision Planning – A Key to the Future

The reason for the preeminent placement of technology testing is that this analysis (of the vision compared to technology projections) is the one analysis that can identify true 'show stoppers' for a draft vision. Most of the other iterative analyses (e.g., market, competitor, etc.) can only yield 'soft' information. (That soft information may still become a reason to change the vision through the exercise of judgment). However, if the technology analysis indicated no likelihood of a needed technology being available any time near the schedule proposed, then that is a very 'hard' change indicator.

Another reason that the technology tests are so important at this early stage is the all pervasiveness of technology in today's economy. Even if the company under consideration is not itself in a technology based industry, the extreme penetration of communications and computers in all phases of virtually all organizations dictates that technology is going to be a major factor in any vision development. In addition, the central roles of communications and computing systems in the re-engineering efforts have made the pervasiveness of these forms of technology and their importance still greater. Even with totally non-tech industries (examples are hard to develop, but maybe some of the hand-craft industries are close), distribution channels, promotion, billing, service access, etc. are all likely to be highly dependent on technology and technology developments.

In trying to make an evaluation of the technology match, it is necessary to develop an idea of the required technology for the vision and of the technology that will be available in the future time of concern. A straightforward comparison is then made. A more detailed discussion of this process follows, and this may be taken as a template for other tests.

Technology projection test

In this test, it is necessary to analyze the projected needs of the vision in terms of technology in the future. The types of technology and the levels of the technology needed to achieve the vision must be determined.vii Also the timing of the need and the application of the technology must be understood and

developed in an informal manner. This statement of needs must then be compared to the best available information regarding the availability of the technology as to both type and schedule.

If the vision requires technology that is not projected to be available, do we then change the vision? No! It is not necessarily time to make any changes yet; it is time to utilize judgment. If there is only a relatively small discrepancy (say a needed technology is projected to be available a year after it is needed), then that suggests that part of the Vision Planning process needs to address accelerating the availability of the technology. (Of course, such acceleration may not always be practical or possible, but that is part of the use of judgment.) However, if the vision dictates the use of a technology in five years that present analysis suggests would require re-writing the laws of physics, then it is time to modify the vision.

Other Tests

In addition to the technology tests, it is necessary to also test the vision against other appropriate yardsticks. Which are these? That largely depends on the nature of the industry and vision in question. Certainly some economic measurement needs to be made. This implies that some kind of costs vs. income estimates must be made and an evaluation made as to the payoff.

It may not be possible to make the somewhat highly detailed comparison to alternatives that are more traditional in planning activities. To see why these kinds of comparisons may not be possible consider the vision statements that we have thus far encountered:

Vision Planning – A Key to the Future

Lincoln – "...preservation of the Union in the same form."

Not attributed – "... our software will be preeminent in its field by the year 2000 as demonstrated by its use by at least five of the ten largest companies in the industry."

Gerstner – "... be the world's most important and successful information technology company."

Entertainment Company – "Keep the mascot in front of the people."

Just from inspection of these vision statements, it should be apparent that a quantitative evaluation against alternatives is not generally practical. Defining alternatives is the problem. What would be the alternative to any of the above that would make for a meaningful evaluation?

Lincoln – "Preserve part of the Union?"

Not attributed – "Our software will be good but not preeminent?"

Gerstner – "Be the world's second most important and successful information company?"

Entertainment Company – "Keep the mascot in front of some of the people (or some of the time)?"

No! None of these makes sense as alternative visions, and consequently a detailed economic evaluation of alternatives is not possible. Later in the process there will be a very distinct need for those detailed evaluating (in the Backwards Deployment step.)

So again, the use of judgment is needed to determine if projected bottom line impact makes a vision worthwhile. In addition judgment is needed to determine how far to go (how much detail) in developing cost and revenue projections. It is

likely that anything more than the broadest measures at this point are a waste of time; distracting to the real intent of the process; and possibly misleading.

Other areas that should be used for tests depend strongly on the industry under consideration. Some possibilities are:

- Potential regulatory changes or responses for regulated business,
- Possible legal changes,
- Possible new market entrants,
- Possible competitor actions and or responses, etc.

Each of these should be reviewed as well as other yardsticks important to a specific organization.

Step 3. Restatement

After each of these reviews, appropriate modifications should be made to the vision. As noted before, while this is the time to bring the vision in to the realm of feasibility, it is important that the leader throughout this process stress the need to have a vision that will be difficult. The perfect vision would be one that is just marginally feasible.

Step 4. Backwards deployment.

This rather strange sounding term is the real 'pay-off' stage of Vision Planning. It could be called migration plan development or high level implementation planning, but the term 'backwards deployment' is much more descriptive of the activity. By 'backward deployment' is meant the process of starting with the future vision and working backwards in time to

Vision Planning – A Key to the Future

today's reality. In so doing a road map -- a high level implementation plan -- is prepared to guide later, more detailed strategic and implementation planning.

This is called the pay-off stage because the goal of any planning activity is to determine what actions should be taken today to reach tomorrow's goals and that is precisely what happens in this stage. The genius of Vision Planning is that it starts with a desired future, rather than starting with the present and merely projecting it forward. One is thus able to 'invent the future'.

The approach to this stage is to visualize the future desired state and to work backwards in time in large increments, determining what each preceding logical step(s) would be. It is here that traditional economic evaluations of alternatives should be used to select the 'best' of these steps. This activity results in the high-level road map. The real skill in this process is tying into the present in the most graceful manner. This tie-in will require the assistance of those highly skilled in today's operation. In addition to the road map, this process should produce lists of characteristics of the operations of the company at major steps along the way. These lists provide an ongoing measurement point as the vision is pursued.

A primary purpose of this stage of Vision Planning activity is to develop solid guidelines and measurements for the following planning and implementation stages. The road map and other outputs should be taken and directly used by the next planning stage. It is important that each stage does not 're-invent the wheel' or the final plans may be unrelated to the vision.

Backwards Deployment Example – Texas Development

An example of the idea of Backwards Deployment comes from the public/corporate combined policy arena. In 1987 before the technology development that now so marks the central part of Texas from Dallas/Fort Worth to San Antonio, Dr. George Kozmetskyviii spoke publiclyix of the future nature of the world and national economies. He was the founder and CEO of a major technology firm, so many listened, but at the time, it was hard to imagine. Dr. Kozmetsky foresaw a world economy based on sustained productivity, adaptability, flexibility, high quality product, and technology diversification. This was Dr. Kozmetsky's statement of his vision of the future world economy (stated, incidentally, in much more eloquent terms than this rapid summary.)

The next step in Dr. Kozmetsky's presentation was the key to the importance of this example. He proceeded to review each major business/geographic section of Texas and to postulate how that section would (could) play an important role in his vision of the future economy. He correctly predicted the establishment of the vast telecommunications development in the Dallas area. This projection was made before GTE, Northern Telecom or the many others had moved to the area. He predicted the development of the Austin area as a computer center. He did this before anyone heard of Dell Computer. He also foresaw the major pharmaceutical establishment developing at the southern end of this technological 'Fertile Crescent' in San Antonio.

That Dr. Kozmetsky was correct in many of his predictions can not be denied. He was also right in predicting the importance of this vision and its associated implementation steps could have for Texas. Technology jobs (predominantly of the types predicted by Dr. Kozmetsky) now represent a major and growing percentage of all Texas employment. In addition, that type employment is growing faster in Texas than in any other state, and that it was growing twice as fast in Texas as overall employment.

The amazing thing about the speech that Dr. Kozmetsky gave on this subject, however, was not the fact of his correct prediction of the development. Rather, it was the way he was able to detail the steps in making it happen. He described many

Vision Planning – A Key to the Future

of the major steps that would be needed to bring the dream to reality. In doing so, he suggested the part each could be playing in 50 years and then he outlined steps that could be taken by both the public and private sectors to reach those positions.

Learning from the Example

- To give Visions the power to affect the future, they must be accompanied by an outline of the details to make them happen.

- To give a Vision the most power over the future, it is necessary to develop the implementing steps in 'backwards' order, i.e., from the future Vision backwards to today's reality. To go the other way ties the future to today's reality, rather than to the desired future Vision.

Things to do in this lesson.

- Review assigned projects from the last lesson.
- What is the best way to fit the Vision Planning Pyramid to this Organization's planning process?
- Make a 'Top Ten' list of the main advantages of Vision Planning.
- Have each participant state and defend his proposed vision statement for the organization.
- Select the top three Vision Statements.
- Each participant should provide his/her top three attributes (in one word, or very few words) of a vision statement. Use this list to develop an agreed on list of 5-10 attributes.
- What areas are the most important for this organization to test against? Why
- How can data for these tests be obtained?
- Can the group agree on a single vision statement from this exercise? What is the best compromise that can be reached?

- How does the new proposed Vision Statement compare to the previously established list of desirable attributes for a Vision Statement?
- How does Backwards Deployment fit with the organization's current planning structure? How can this stage be crafted to fit into a revised Planning Model?
- How can a planning continuity be established so that there is a clear connection between Direction and Implementation as well as a feedback path for measurement of actually achieved objectives against the directions established through the Vision Planning process?
- What will be the important measurements generated in Backwards Deployment for your organization?
- Develop an example of Backwards Deployment that fits your organization.

Assignments for the next lesson.

1. After thought and review of this lesson, develop a restatement of the proposed Vision Statement.
2. Develop a one-sentence statement of the difference
between Vision Planning and traditional strategic planning.
3. Determine the necessary changes (top three) to integrate Vision Planning in to the organization's planning process.
4. Read material for the next lesson.

Vision Planning – A Key to the Future

Lesson 4 – INTEGRATING VISION PLANNING

Lesson Outline

- Understanding the difference between Vision Planning and Strategic Planning.
- Updating the Planning Model.
- Determining how to integrate Vision Planning in to the Organization's planning process.
- Summarizing the overall series of lessons.

Prerequisites for this lesson.

(Now is the time to bring together all of the lessons and to decide how to move forward.)
Completion of lessons 1, 2 and 3.

Completion of assignments from Lesson 3.

Review of material for this lesson and of all previous lessons.

Clifford Holliday

Lesson introduction

This lesson will focus on how to integrate the Vision Planning concepts in to the organization's planning structure. Most of this work will be organization specific, and thus less verbiage is included than in the other lessons. The keys to this lesson are in the "Things to Do" list. It will be through these items that the vision planning process will be implemented in your organization.

How Is Vision Planning Different from Strategic Planning?

Before trying to integrate Vision Planning into the organization's planning structure, it is vitally important to have a clear understanding of the differences between Vision Planning and Strategic Planning. The material in Lesson 2 developed the intellectual differences between these two, but the real world is often more instructive. The following example should clearly bring out these differences.

Lincoln Vision Example – Continued

This continues the vision example of Lincoln started in the first lesson. The purposes of the extension of this example are to illustrate the difference between vision and strategy; to show the importance of continuity in carrying out the strategies and tactics to properly implement the vision; and to understand how alternative strategies support or fail to support the vision.

Vision Planning – A Key to the Future

Lincoln's vision, as was earlier documented, was very simply to preserve the Union in the form that it had been before the war. In order to achieve this vision it was necessary to win

the Civil War by defeating the South. The South on the other hand, was in a position of needing only to stalemate the Union's military attempts -- a victory was not necessary to achieve their goals of maintaining a separate country. Lincoln went through a long series of generals before he finally found a general -- Grant -- who understood and supported his vision. Unlike his predecessors, Grant did not retreat when he experienced defeat by Lee (as he did in almost every battle until the very end). Instead, he maneuvered so as to keep his army in the field and in position to pursue the needed strategy and supporting tactics to achieve Lincoln's vision.

Grant's execution of this strategy resulted in a series of 'sidesteps' after defeats at The Wilderness, at Spotsylvania, at North Anna River and finally at Cold Harbor. These were tactical, and to some extent, strategic disasters for Grant, losing in these battles a number of men approximately equal to the entire Confederate forces. However he continued, understanding the importance of ending the war (i.e., the importance of pursuing the vision). "For the first time in his Civil War experience, Robert E. Lee faced an adversary who had the determination to press on despite the cost."x Ultimately Grant's final sidestep put him in Petersburg, which cut off the Southern rail network and support from the deep south states, eventually resulting in the evacuation of Richmond and the collapse of the Confederacy in early 1865.

Another General -- George B. McClellan -- had a similar opportunity in 1862, but did not understand the vision well enough to take advantage of it. McClellan was on the Richmond - Yorktown Peninsula with an army of well over 120,000 men (at least two and one half times the size of the Southern armies). This was nearly the same place that Grant was two bloody years later after his defeat at Cold Harbor. Here McClellan also ran into R.E.Lee and suffered a defeat at Mechanicsville.

The same tactic that Grant used later was available to McClellan -- he could have sidestepped the Confederate Army at Richmond by falling on Petersburg. Instead, he elected to retreat and protect his army for a later battle. Had he moved instead to Petersburg, it would have had the same effect in 1862 that it had in 1865. The Deep South would have been taken out of the War; the rail network would have been useless; and the South would have had to abandon Richmond. This would have almost surely ended the War -- only over two years, and hundreds of thousands of casualties, earlier.

Learning from the Example

- The leader and the organization (Lincoln and the Union) had a consistent, clear vision.
- One general understood the vision and was willing to support it with appropriate (although very difficult) strategy and tactics.
- One general understood the differences between vision and strategy and selected his strategic alternatives from those that would support the vision of his leader.
- The other, although hailed as one of the military geniuses of the time, either did not understand or did not support the vision of his leader. (McClellan ignored the fact that the vision was to win the war and to thus preserve the Union. Instead he substituted his strategy of protecting his army and retreated in the face of his first loss. The result was the tragic extension of the bloodiest war in this country's history.)

Vision Planning – A Key to the Future

Having made the point of the difference between vision and strategy and having illustrated the importance of having planning continuity from vision to strategy selection, we will move to the discussion of the place of strategic planning in the planning model.

Revised Planning Model

This then is the end of the description and the 'how-to' of the Vision Planning process. However, it should be understood that the process itself never ends. It should be a continuing part of the overall planning process. The activities outlined here should be performed every year to assure that the vision stays 'fresh' in terms of the ever changing market and technology characteristics. The following section redefines the previously presented Planning Model.

Clifford Holliday

THE PLANNING MODEL

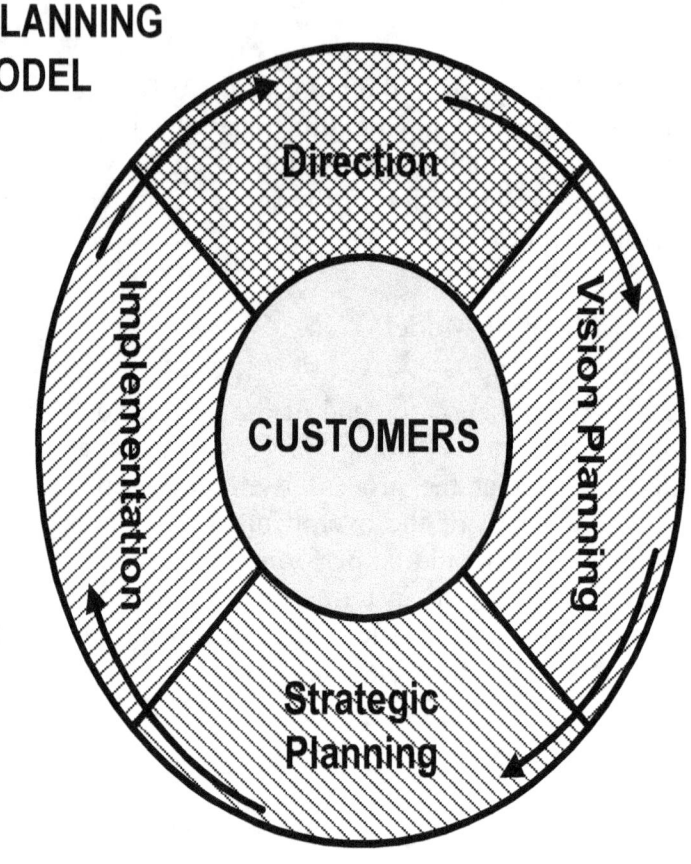

(C) 1998 B & C Consulting Services

Figure 6, Original Planning Model

This is the same model that was developed in the first lesson on the overall planning process. With this model in place, diagrammatically it is only necessary to insert the Vision

Planning Pyramid (see Figure 2 in Lesson 2) to develop the integrated approach. While this is simple on paper, it may be far more complicated in actual practice. The 'Things to do in this lesson' sidebar, is intended to lead the user to the integration in

Vision Planning – A Key to the Future

his   organization.

Revised Model

The work in this Lesson has enhanced the original model and it now has the following form;

Figure 7. Planning Model with Vision Planning Expanded

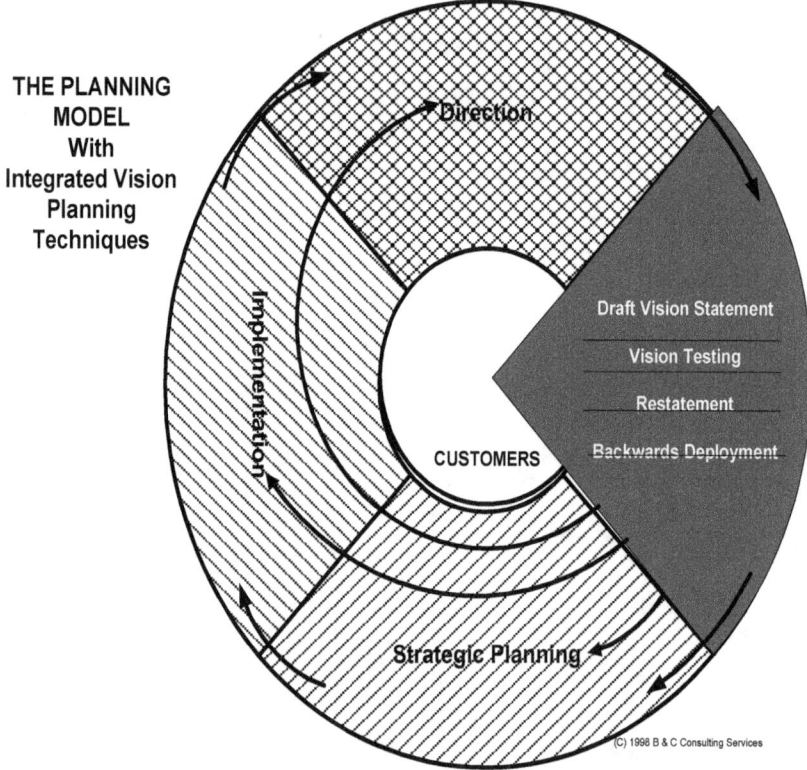

Vision Planning – A Key to the Future

The view of the Planning Model now incorporates the developed detail of the lessons since the establishment of the Planning Framework. While the differences in this model may seem small, they are very significant:

The Vision Planning 'box' has now been replaced with the Vision Planning Pyramid representing the entire Vision Planning process.

There are now multiple ties from the Vision Planning system to other parts of the planning system.

There is a tie directly to Strategic Planning that suggests the use of the 'Backwards Deployment' steps to define major activities in the Strategic Plan.

There is a direct tie to Implementation from 'Backwards Deployment' (BD) to identify the use of the major activities identified in BD as implementation steps.

There is a direct tie from the Vision Planning Pyramid back to the Direction box to signify the establishment of measurements of success based on the defined activities in Vision Planning.

Integration Example – School District

The author has worked on several occasions for a major school district (K-12 with over 170,000 students). One of the earliest identified problems was their lack of a Vision. To be more accurate they had several Visions. At an early meeting with the Superintendent and several members of his top planning staff, the consultant asked what their Vision was for the school District. There were several replies as to what the Vision was but they were all different. This was symptomatic of many of their problems with multiple competing directions (see material concerning Direction in Lesson 1.) They decided to approach their problems by pursuing a version of the Vision Planning process over a period of several years.

The school district developed a Vision that reminds one of the "Mascot" Vision in its brevity. Theirs was (is, actually) "Any time, Any Place, Any One." This statement refers to the ability for any one in the system (student, teacher, and administrator) to be able to access the appropriate educational and/or administrative system and resources from any place at any time. This very ambitions Vision was not at all possible in their existing technology environment. To address it they decided that they needed a 'technology architecture'. This was to be their guiding statement as to the selection of technology directions as they went forward. In the terms of Vision Planning it was their 'Backwards Deployment' Plan. They enfolded that plan in to their overall planning process, and used it in conjunction with all of their planning activities. While this is not a perfect integration, it has proven to be a very usable method.

Learning from the Example

The school system's high administrators each thought they had a Vision guiding their efforts. The problem was that they had different Vision. There was no overall integration of the planning effort.

If that function had been working as described herein, then the lack of movement towards the desired Vision would have been apparent.

Integration of Vision Planning can take many forms from the very formal approach indicated in Figure 7 to the much more informal approach of the school district. The individual organization must decide what will work best in their circumstances.

Summary

The following thoughts are offered to help state the most important points of this entire manual.

Vision Planning – A Key to the Future

- Vision is an essential quality for a great leader and for great organizations.

- A vision of the future can allow a leader and/or an organization to 'invent' the future.

- Vision statements, the driving force of Vision Planning, are a balance between the very difficult and the possible.

- Good visions are :
  clear,
  concise,
  communicable,
  communicated,
  measurable,
  inspiring,
  challenging,
  <u>but feasible.</u>

- Vision Planning is a process of iteration based on a continued series of tests and restatement.

- The main components of the Vision Planning process are vision development, testing, restatement, and Backwards Deployment.

- Backwards Deployment will provide a basis for tying all the other parts of the planning process together.

- It is necessary to revise the organization's planning process in order to incorporate Vision Planning.

- The entire process of Vision Planning and the planning process itself must be driven by the head of the organization.

Things to do in this lesson.

Review the revised Vision Statements from the 'Assignments'. Can the group now agree on what every one will consider an excellent Vision Statement and one that the leader will accept and endorse? If not a separate session is indicated as outlined in Lesson 3.

Review the lists of changes needed to integrate vision planning (from Assignments). Develop a 'top ten' to-do list of the needed changes.

Can this set of changes be implemented? If not, what has to be done to achieve implementation? If they can be done, what is the needed first step? Who is responsible for this first step?

Develop the new planning model for the organization. Do a very simple one to start, and when it is perfected, add detail.

If not already covered, determine the parts of the organization with primary responsibility for each of the steps of Vision Planning. Determine who has the overall responsibility for Vision Planning.

Vision Planning – A Key to the Future

Endnotes

[i] B & C Consulting Services (c.holliday@ieee.org) is specifically designed to offer these services on a selected customer basis. Web Site: http:// crhollidaycom.wordpress.com

[ii] From Lincoln's address to the special session of Congress on July 4, 1861.

[iii] Lincoln's Gettysburg Address.

[iv] Burgess, John, "Gerstner Defends His IBM Vision," Dallas Morning News, March 25, 1994, Section d, page 1 -10.

[v] Ibid

[vi] It should be noted that this last dictate is not in conflict with earlier comments about the lack of detail involved in the formation of a vision statement. This statement from Peter's is really concerned with the continual focus on the vision as it is "lived", i.e., implemented.

[vii] It should be noted that at this stage all "determinations" are intended to be very broad in nature. Any attempt to refine these projections to the kind of detail that would guide day-to-day decisions would be wasteful and probably destructive to the entire process.

[viii] Dr. Kozmetsky was Director of the IC2 Institute of the University of Texas, Austin, Texas, Professor of Management and Computer Sciences, and Executive Associate for Economic Affairs.

[ix] Dr. Kozmetsky's speech was delivered to the Texas-Japan Association Conference, Oita, Japan September 7, 1987. It is identified as "Working Paper #87-9-1.

[x] Quoted by many Civil War authors.

www.ingramcontent.com/pod-product-compliance
Lightning Source LLC
Chambersburg PA
CBHW070957240526
45469CB00016B/1534